The Historic, Mythic and Mystic Christ

By Annie Besant

ISBN: 978-1-63118-533-5

Esoteric Classics

Other Books in this Series and Related Titles

The Use of Evil by Annie Besant (978-1-63118-532-8)

Aurora of the Philosophers by Paracelsus (978-1-63118-507-6)

Clairvoyance and Psychic Abilities by A Besant &c (978-1-63118-403-1)

The Feminine Occult by various authors (978-1-63118-711-7)

Rosicrucian Rules, Secret Signs, Codes and Symbols by various (978-1-63118-488-8)

An Outline of Theosophy by C W Leadbeater (978-1-63118-452-9)

Paracelsus, the Four Elements and Their Spirits by M P Hall (978-1-63118-400-0)

The Stone of the Philosophers by A E Waite (978-1-63118-509-0)

Essays on the Esoteric Tradition of Karma by A Besant &c (978-1-63118-426-0)

The Rosicrucian Chemical Marriage by Christian Rosenkreuz (978-1-63118-458-1)

The Alchemical Catechism of Paracelsus by Paracelsus (978-1-63118-513-7)

Alchemy in the Nineteenth Century by Helena P Blavatsky (978-1-63118-446-8)

Qabbalistic Teachings and the Tree of Life by M P Hall (978-1-63118-482-6)

The Devil in Love by Jacques Cazotte (978–1–63118–499–4)

History, Analysis and Secret Tradition of the Tarot by Hall &c (978-1-63118-445-1)

Crystal Vision Through Crystal Gazing by Frater Achad (978-1-63118-455-0)

The Golden Verses of Pythagoras: Five Translations (978-1-63118-479-6)

Arcane Formulas or Mental Alchemy by W W Atkinson (978-1-63118-459-8)

The Machinery of the Mind by Dion Fortune (978-1-63118-451-2)

The A E Waite Reader: A Selection of Occult Essays (978-1-63118-515-1)

The Leadbeater Reader: A Selection of Occult Essays (978-1-63118-483-3)

Audio versions are also available on Audible, Amazon and Apple

Other Books in this Series and Related Titles

On the Cave of the Nymphs in the Odyssey by Thomas Taylor (978-1-63118-505-2)

Occult Symbolism of Animals, Insects, Reptiles, Fish & Birds (978-1-63118-420-8)

The Poem of Hashish by A Crowley & C Baudelaire (978-1-63118-484-0)

Brothers & Builders by Joseph Fort Newton (978-1-63118-506-9)

The Kabbalah of Masonry & Related Writings by E Levi &c (978-1-63118-453-6)

A Collection of Fiction and Essays by Occult Writers on Supernatural and Metaphysical Subjects by various (978–1–63118–510–6)

The Sepher Yetzirah and the Qabalah by M P Hall (978-1-63118-481-9)

Cloud Upon the Sanctuary by Waite & K Eckartshausen (978-1-63118-438-3)

The Hymns of Hermes by G R S Mead (978-1-63118-405-5)

The Secrets of Enoch by Enoch (978-1-63118-449-9)

Masonic and Rosicrucian History by M P Hall & H Voorhis (978-1-63118-486-4)

The Sword of Welleran and Other Stories by Lord Dunsany (978-1-63118-501-4)

The Eleusinian Mysteries and Rites by Dudley Wright (978–1–63118–530–4)

Gnosis of the Mind by G. R. S. Mead (978-1-63118-408-6)

The First and Second Gospels of the Infancy of Jesus Christ (978-1-63118-415-4)

The Life of Pythagoras by Porphyry (978-1-63118-512-0)

Freemasonry & Catholicism by Max Heindel (978-1-63118-508-3)

Rosicrucians and Speculative Masonry in the Seventeenth Century (978-1-63118-489-5)

The Influence of Pythagoras on Freemasonry and Other Essays (978-1-63118-404-8)

The Path of Light: A Manual of Maha-Yana Buddhism (978-1-63118-471-0)

Tao Te Ching & Commentary by Lao Tzu & C Johnston (978-1-63118-495-6)

Audio versions are also available on Audible, Amazon and Apple

Table of Contents

INTRODUCTION

The word "esoteric" can be difficult to define. Esotericism in general can be seen less as a system of beliefs and more as a category, which encompasses numerous, different systems of beliefs. It's a bit of juxtaposition, since the word "esoteric" indicates something that few people know about, while the term itself broadly covers numerous philosophies, practices, areas of study and belief systems.

In a greater sense, Esotericism acts as a storehouse for secret knowledge, which is often considered ancient (by *tradition, if not by fact),* passed down from generation to generation, in private. At various times in history, simply possessing the knowledge of some of these subjects, was considered illegal and a jailable offence, if discovered. This usually included such general topics as Alchemy, Pharmacology, Qabalah, Hermeticism, Occultism, Ceremonial Magic, Astrology, Divination, Rosicrucianism and so on. Collectively, these areas of study were often referred to as the esoteric sciences.

Sometimes, the outer garment of a subject isn't esoteric, while what is hidden beneath it, is. As an example, Freemasonry isn't necessarily esoteric by nature (at *least not anymore),* but certain signs, passwords and handshakes given to the candidate during their initiation, are in fact, esoteric, in the sense that they are hidden from the general public.

Today, in the twenty-first century, such topics are readily available at bookstores across the country, and numerous mainsteam publishers offer beginners guides and coffee-table volumes on many of these subjects, intended for mass appeal. Books like "*The Secret*" have turned previously arcane topics into household knowledge. All that being the case, however, it isn't to say that there still aren't buried secrets to uncover, ancient wisdom being ignored and forgotten mysteries to be explored. In fact, it is often that we are only able to further our own studies by standing on the shoulders of these disappearing giants.

Lamp of Trismegistus is doing its part to help preserve humanity's esoteric history by making some of these classics available to those students who are seeking to unearth the knowledge of these ancient colossi.

So, be sure to check other titles from our *Esoteric Classics* series, as well as our *Occult Fiction*, *Theosophical Classics*, *Foundations of Freemasonry Series*, *Supernatural Fiction*, *Paranormal Research Series*, *Studies in Buddhism* and our *Christian Apocrypha Series.* You can also download the audio versions of most of these titles from Amazon, Apple or Audible, for learning on the go.

THE HISTORICAL CHRIST

It is no doubt that throughout the identities existing across all the religions of the world, we are able to see that through a study of these identities, beliefs, symbolisms, rites, ceremonies, histories, and commemorative festivals, has arisen a modern school which relates the whole of these to a common source in human ignorance, and in a primitive explanation of natural phenomena. From these identities have been drawn weapons for the stabbing of each religion in turn, and the most effective attacks on Christianity and on the historical existence of its Founder have been armed from this source. On entering now on the study of the life of the Christ, of the rites of Christianity, its sacraments, its doctrines, it would be fatal to ignore the facts marshalled by Comparative Mythologists. Rightly understood, they may be made serviceable instead of mischievous. We have seen that the Apostles and their successors dealt very freely with the Old Testament as having an allegorical and mystic sense far more important than the historical, though by no means negating it, and that they did not scruple to teach the instructed believer that some of the stories that were apparently historical were really purely allegorical. Nowhere, perhaps, is it more necessary to understand this than when we are studying the story of Jesus, surnamed the Christ, for when we do not disentangle the intertwisted threads, and see where symbols have been taken as events, allegories as histories, we lose most of the instructiveness of the narrative and much of its rarest beauty. We cannot too much insist on the fact that Christianity gains, it does not lose, when knowledge is added to faith and virtue, according to the apostolic injunction. Men fear that Christianity will be weakened when reason studies it, and that it is "dangerous" to admit that events thought to be historical have the deeper significance of the mythical or mystical meaning. It is, on the contrary, strengthened, and the student finds, with joy, that the pearl of great price shines with a purer, clearer lustre when the coating of ignorance is removed and its many colours are seen.

There are two schools of thought at the present time, bitterly opposed to each other, who dispute over the story of the great Hebrew Teacher. According to one school there is nothing at all in the accounts of His life save myths and legends — myths and legends that were given as explanations of certain natural phenomena, survivals of a pictorial way of teaching certain facts of nature, of impressing on the minds of the uneducated certain grand classifications of natural events that were important in themselves, and that lent themselves to moral instruction. Those who endorse this view form a well-defined school to which belong many men of high education and strong intelligence, and round them gather crowds of the less instructed, who emphasise with crude vehemence the more destructive elements in their pronouncements. This school is opposed by that of the believers in orthodox Christianity, who declare that the whole story of Jesus is history, unadulterated by legend or myth. They maintain that this history is nothing more than the history of the life of a man born some nineteen centuries ago in Palestine, who passed through all the experiences set down in the Gospels, and they deny that the story has any significance beyond that of a divine and human life. These two schools stand in direct antagonism, one asserting that everything is legend, the other declaring that everything is history. Between them lie many phases of opinion generally labelled "freethinking", which regard the life-story as partly legendary and partly historical, but offer no definite and rational method of interpretation, no adequate explanation of the complex whole. And we also find, within the limits of the Christian Church, a large and ever-increasing number of faithful and devout Christians of refined intelligence, men and women who are earnest in their faith and religious in their aspirations, but who see in the Gospel story more than the history of a single divine Man, They allege — defending their position from the received Scriptures — that the story of the Christ has a deeper and more significant meaning than lies on the surface; while they maintain the historical character of Jesus, they at the same time declare that THE CHRIST is more than the man Jesus, and has a mystical meaning. In support of this contention they point to such phrases as that used by S. Paul: "My little children, of whom I travail in birth again until Christ be formed in you"; here S. Paul obviously cannot refer to a historical Jesus, but to some forth-putting from the human soul which is to him the shaping of Christ therein. Again the same teacher declares that though he had known Christ after the flesh yet from henceforth he would know him thus no more; obviously implying that while he recognised the Christ of the flesh — Jesus — there was a higher view to which he had attained which threw into the shade the historical Christ. This is the view which many are seeking in our own days, and — faced by the facts of Comparative Religion, puzzled by the contradictions of the Gospels, confused by problems they cannot solve so long as they are tied down to the mere surface meanings of their Scripture — they cry despairingly that the letter killeth while the spirit giveth life, and seek to trace some deep and wide significance in a story which is as old as the religions of the world, and has always served as the very centre and life of every religion in which it has reappeared. These struggling thinkers, too unrelated and indefinite to be spoken of as forming a school, seem to stretch out a hand on one side to those who think that all is legend, asking them to accept a historical basis; on the other side they say to their fellow Christians that there is a growing danger lest, in clinging to a literal and unique meaning, which cannot be defended before the increasing knowledge of the day, the spiritual meaning should be entirely lost. There is a danger of losing "the story of the Christ," with that thought of the Christ which has been the support and inspiration of millions of noble lives in East and West, though the Christ be called by other names and worshipped under other forms; a danger lest the pearl of great price should escape from our hold, and man be left the poorer for evermore.

What is needed, in order that this danger may be averted, is to disentangle the different threads in the story of the Christ, and to lay them side by side — the thread of history, the thread of legend, the thread of mysticism. These have been intertwined into a single strand, to the great loss of the thoughtful, and in disentangling them we shall find that the story becomes more, not less, valuable as knowledge is added to it, and that here, as in all that is basically of the truth, the brighter the light thrown upon it the greater the beauty that is revealed.

We will study first the historical Christ; secondly, the mythic Christ; thirdly, the mystic Christ. And we shall find that elements drawn from all these make up the Jesus Christ of the Churches. They all enter into the composition of the grandiose and pathetic Figure which dominates the thoughts and the emotions of Christendom, the Man of Borrows, the Saviour, the Lover and Lord of Men.

THE HISTORICAL CHRIST
OR
JESUS THE HEALER AND TEACHER

The thread of the life-story of Jesus is one which may be disentangled from those with which it is intertwined without any great difficulty. We may fairly here aid our study by reference to those records of the past which experts can reverify for themselves, and from which certain details regarding the Hebrew Teacher have been given to the world by H. P. Blavatsky and by others who are experts in occult investigation. Now in the minds of many there is apt to arise a challenge when this word "expert" is used in connection with occultism. Yet it only means a person who by special study, by special training, has accumulated a special kind of knowledge, and has developed powers that enable him to give an opinion founded on his own individual knowledge of the subject with which he is dealing. Just as we speak of Huxley as an expert in biology, as we speak of a Senior Wrangler as an expert in mathematics, or of Lyell as an expert in geology, so we may fairly call a man an expert in occultism who has first mastered intellectually certain fundamental theories of the constitution of man and the universe, and secondly has developed within himself the powers that are latent in everyone — and are capable of being developed by those who give themselves to appropriate studies — capacities which enable him to examine for himself the more obscure processes of nature. As a man may be born with a mathematical faculty, and by training that faculty year after year may immensely increase his mathematical capacity, so may a man be born with certain faculties within him, faculties belonging to the Soul, which he can develop by training and by discipline. When, having developed those faculties, he applies them to the study of the invisible world, such a man becomes an expert in Occult Science, and such a man can at his will reverify the records to which I have referred. Such reverification is as much out of the reach of the ordinary person as a mathematical book written in the symbols of the higher mathematics is out of the reach of those who are untrained in mathematical science. There is nothing exclusive in the knowledge save as every science is exclusive; those who are born with a faculty, and train the faculty, can master its appropriate science, while those who start in life without any faculty, or those who do not develop it if they have it, must be content to remain in ignorance. These are the rules everywhere of the obtaining of knowledge, in Occultism as in every other science.

The occult records partly endorse the story told in the Gospels, and partly do not endorse it; they show us the life, and thus enable us to disentangle it from the myths which are intertwined therewith.

The child whose Jewish name has been turned into that of Jesus was born in Palestine B.C. 105, during the consulate of Publius Rutilius Rufus and Gnaeus Mallius Maximus. His parents were well-born though poor, and he was educated in a knowledge of the Hebrew Scriptures. His fervent devotion and a gravity beyond his years led his parents to dedicate him to the religious and ascetic life, and soon after a visit to Jerusalem, in which the extraordinary intelligence and eagerness for knowledge of the youth were shown in his seeking of the doctors in the Temple, he was sent to be trained in an Essene community in the southern Judaean desert. When he had reached the age of nineteen he went on to the Essene monastery near Mount Serbal, a monastery which was much visited by learned men travelling from Persia and India to Egypt, and where a magnificent library of occult works — many of them Indian of the Trans-Himalayan regions — had been established. From this seat of mystic learning he proceeded later to Egypt. He had been fully instructed in the secret teachings which were the real fount of life among the Essenes, and was initiated in Egypt as a disciple of that one sublime Lodge from which every great religion has its Founder. For Egypt has remained one of the world-centres of the true Mysteries, whereof all semi-public Mysteries are the faint and far-off reflections. The Mysteries spoken of in history as Egyptian were the shadows of the true things "in the Mount", and there the young Hebrew received the solemn consecration which prepared him for the Royal Priesthood he was later to attain. So superhumanly pure and so full of devotion was he, that in his gracious manhood he stood out pre-eminently from the severe and somewhat fanatical ascetics among whom he had been trained, shedding on the stern Jews around him the fragrance of a gentle and tender wisdom, as a rose-tree strangely planted in a desert would shed its sweetness on the barrenness around. The fair and stately grace of his white purity was round him as a radiant moonlit halo, and his words, though few, were ever sweet and loving, winning even the most harsh to a temporary gentleness, and the most rigid to a passing softness. Thus he lived through nine-and-twenty years of mortal life, growing from grace to grace.

This superhuman purity and devotion fitted the man Jesus, the disciple, to become the temple of a loftier Power, of a mighty, indwelling Presence. The time had come for one of those Divine manifestations which from age to age are made for the helping of humanity, when a new impulse is needed to quicken the spiritual evolution of mankind, when a new civilisation is about to dawn. The world of the West was then in the womb of time, ready for the birth, and the Teutonic sub-race was to catch the sceptre of empire falling from the failing hands of Rome. Ere it started on its journey a World-Saviour must appear, to stand in blessing beside the cradle of the infant Hercules.

A mighty "Son of God" was to take flesh upon earth, a supreme Teacher, "full of grace and truth" — One in whom the Divine Wisdom abode in fullest measure, who was verily "the Word" incarnate, Light and Life in outpouring richness, a very Fountain of the Waters of Life. Lord of Compassion and of Wisdom — such was His name — and from His dwelling in the Secret Places He came forth into the world of men.

For Him was needed an earthly tabernacle, a human form, the body of a man, and who so fit to yield his body in glad and willing service to One before whom Angels and men bow down in lowliest reverence, as this Hebrew of the Hebrews, this purest and noblest of "the Perfect", whose spotless body and stainless mind offered the best that humanity could bring ? The man Jesus yielded himself a willing sacrifice, "offered himself without spot" to the Lord of Love, who took unto Himself that pure form as tabernacle, and dwelt therein for three years of mortal life.

This epoch is marked in the traditions embodied in the Gospels as that of the Baptism of Jesus, when the Spirit was seen "descending from heaven like a dove, and it abode upon Him", and a celestial voice proclaimed Him as the beloved Son, to whom men should give ear. Truly was He the beloved Son in whom the Father was well-pleased, and from that time forward "Jesus began to preach", and was that wondrous mystery, "God manifest in the flesh" — not unique in that He was God, for: "Is it not written in your law, I said, Ye are Gods ? If he called them Gods, unto whom the word of God came, and the scripture cannot be broken; say ye of Him, whom the Father hath sanctified and sent into the world, Thou blasphemest; because I said, I am the Son of God ?" Truly all men are Gods, in respect to the Spirit within them, but not in all is the Godhead manifested, as in that well-beloved Son of the Most High.

To that manifested Presence the name of "the Christ" may rightly be given, and it was He who lived and moved in the form of the man Jesus over the hills and plains of Palestine, teaching, healing diseases, and gathering round Him as disciples a few of the more advanced souls. The rare charm of His royal love, outpouring from Him as rays from a sun, drew round Him the suffering, the weary, and the oppressed, and the subtly tender magic of His gentle wisdom purified, ennobled, and sweetened the lives that came into contact with His own. By parable and luminous imagery He taught the uninstructed crowds who pressed around Him, and, using the powers of the free Spirit, He healed many a disease by word or touch, reinforcing the magnetic energies belonging to His pure body with the compelling force of His inner life. Rejected by His Essene brethren among whom He first laboured — whose arguments against His purposed life of loving labour are summarised in the story of the temptation — because he carried to the people the spiritual wisdom that they regarded as their proudest and most secret treasure, and because His all-embracing love drew within its circle the outcast and the degraded — ever loving in the lowest as in the highest, the Divine Self — He saw gathering round Him all too quickly the dark clouds of hatred and suspicion. The teachers and rulers of His nation soon came to eye Him with jealousy and anger; His spirituality was a constant reproach to their materialism, His power a constant, though silent, exposure of their weakness. Three years had scarcely passed since His baptism when the gathering storm outbroke, and the human body of Jesus paid the penalty for enshrining the glorious Presence of a Teacher more than man.

The little band of chosen disciples whom He had selected as repositories of His teachings were thus deprived of their Master's physical presence ere they had assimilated His instructions, but they were souls of high and advanced type, ready to learn the Wisdom, and fit to hand it on to lesser men. Most receptive of all was that "disciple whom Jesus loved", young, eager, and fervid, profoundly devoted to his Master, and sharing His spirit of all-embracing love. He represented, through the century that followed the physical departure of the Christ, the spirit of mystic devotion that sought the exstasis, the vision of and the union with the Divine, while the later great Apostle, S. Paul, represented the wisdom side of the Mysteries.

The Master did not forget His promise to come to them after the world had lost sight of Him, and for something over fifty years He visited them in His subtle spiritual body, continuing the teachings He had begun while with them, and training them in a knowledge of occult truths. They lived together, for the most part, in a retired spot on the outskirts of Judaea, attracting no attention among the many apparently similar communities of the time, studying the profound truths He taught them and acquiring "the gifts of the Spirit".

These inner instructions, commenced during His physical life among them and carried on after He had left the body, formed the basis of the "Mysteries of Jesus", which we have seen in early Church History, and gave the inner life which was the nucleus round which gathered the heterogeneous materials which formed ecclesiastical Christianity.

In the remarkable fragment called the Pistis Sophia, we have a document of the greatest interest bearing on the hidden teaching, written by the famous Valentinus. In this it is said that during the eleven years immediately after His death Jesus instructed His disciples so far as "the regions of the first statutes only, and up to the regions of the first mystery, the mystery within the veil". They had not so far learned the distribution of the angelic orders, of part whereof Ignatius speaks. Then Jesus, being "in the Mount" with His disciples, and having received His mystic Vesture, the knowledge of all the regions and the Words of Power which unlocked them, taught His disciples further, promising: "I will perfect you in every perfection, from the mysteries of the interior to the mysteries of the exterior: I will fill you with the Spirit, so that ye shall be called spiritual, perfect in all perfections". And He taught them of Sophia, the Wisdom, and of her fall into matter in her attempt to rise unto the Highest, and of her cries to the Light in which she had trusted, and of the sending of Jesus to redeem her from chaos, and of her crowning with His light, and leading forth from bondage. And He told them further of the highest Mystery, the ineffable, the simplest and clearest of all, though the highest, to be known by him alone who utterly renounced the world; by that knowledge men became Christs, for such "men are myself, and I am these men", for Christ is that highest Mystery. Knowing that, men are "transformed into pure light and are brought into the light". And He performed for them the great ceremony of Initiation, the baptism "which leadeth to the region of truth and into the region of light", and bade them celebrate it for others who were worthy: "But hide ye this mystery, give it not unto every man, but unto him [only] who shall do all things which I have said unto you in my commandments".

Thereafter, being fully instructed, the apostles went forth to preach, ever aided by their Master.

Moreover these same disciples and their earliest colleagues wrote down from memory all the public sayings and parables of the Master that they had heard, and collected with great eagerness any reports they could find, writing down these also, and circulating them all among those who gradually attached themselves to their small community. Various collections were made, any member writing down what he himself remembered, and adding selections from the accounts of others. The inner teachings, given by the Christ to His chosen ones, were not written down, but were taught orally to those deemed worthy to receive them, to students who formed small communities for leading a retired life, and remained in touch with the central body.

The historical Christ, then, is a glorious Being belonging to the great spiritual hierarchy that guides the spiritual evolution of humanity, who used for some three years the human body of the disciple Jesus; who spent the last of these three years in public teaching throughout Judaea and Samaria; who was a healer of diseases and performed other remarkable occult works; who gathered round Him a small band of disciples whom He instructed in the deeper truths of the spiritual life; who drew men to Him by the singular love and tenderness and the rich wisdom that breathed from His Person; and who was finally put to death for blasphemy, for teaching the inherent Divinity of Himself and of all men. He came to give a new impulse of spiritual life to the world; to re-issue the inner teachings affecting spiritual life; to mark out again the narrow ancient way; to proclaim the existence of the "Kingdom of Heaven", of the Initiation which admits to that knowledge of God which is eternal life; and to admit a few to that Kingdom who should be able to teach others. Round this glorious Figure gathered the myths which united Him to the long array of His predecessors, the myths telling in allegory the story of all such lives, as they symbolise the work of the Logos in the Kosmos and the higher evolution of the individual human soul.

But it must not be supposed that the work of the Christ for His followers was over after He had established the Mysteries, or was confined to rare appearances therein. That Mighty One who had used the body of Jesus as His vehicle, and whose guardian care extends over the whole spiritual evolution of the fifth race of humanity, gave into the strong hands of the holy disciple who had surrendered to Him his body the care of the infant Church.

Perfecting his human evolution, Jesus became one of the Masters of Wisdom, and took Christianity under His special charge, ever seeking to guide it to the right lines, to protect, to guard and nourish it. He was the Hierophant in the Christian Mysteries, the direct Teacher of the Initiates. His the inspiration that kept alight the Gnosis in the Church, until the superincumbent mass of ignorance became so great that even His breath could not fan the flame sufficiently to prevent its extinguishment. His the patient labour which strengthened soul after soul to endure through the darkness, and cherish within itself the spark of mystic longing, the thirst to find the Hidden God. His the steady inpouring of truth into every brain ready to receive it, so that hand stretched out to hand across the centuries and passed on the torch of knowledge, which thus was never extinguished. His the Form which stood beside the rack and in the flames of the burning pile, cheering His confessors and His martyrs, soothing the anguish of their pains, and filling their hearts with His peace. His the impulse which spoke in the thunder of Savonarola, which guided the calm wisdom of Erasmus, which inspired the deep ethics of the God-intoxicated Spinoza. His the energy which impelled Roger Bacon, Galileo, and Paracelsus in their searchings into nature. His the beauty that allured Fra Angelica and Raphael and Leonardo da Vinci, that inspired the genius of Michael-Angelo, that shone before the eyes of Murillo, and that gave the power that raised the marvels of the world, the Duorno of Milan, the San Marco of Venice, the Cathedral of Florence. His the melody that breathed in the masses of Mozart, the sonatas of Beethoven, the oratorios of Handel, the fugues of Bach, the austere splendour of Brahms. His the Presence that cheered the solitary mystics, the hunted occultists, the patient seekers after truth. By persuasion and by menace, by the eloquence of a S. Francis and by the gibes of a Voltaire, by the sweet submission of a Thomas à Kempis, and the rough virility of a Luther, He sought to instruct and awaken, to win into holiness or to scourge from evil. Through the long centuries He has striven and laboured, and, with all the mighty burden of the Churches to carry, He has never left uncared for or unsolaced one human heart that cried to Him for help. And now He is striving to turn to the benefit of Christendom part of the great flood of the Wisdom poured out for the refreshing of the world, and He is seeking through the Churches for some who have ears to hear the Wisdom, and who will answer to His appeal for messengers to carry it to His flock; "Here am I; send me".

THE MYTHIC CHRIST

We have already seen the use that is made of Comparative Mythology against Religion, and some of its most destructive attacks have been levelled against the Christ. His birth of a Virgin at "Christmas", the slaughter of the Innocents, His wonder-working and His teachings, His crucifixion, resurrection, and ascension — all these events in the story of His life are pointed to in the stories of other lives, and His historical existence is challenged on the strength of these identities. So far as the wonder-working and the teachings are concerned, we may briefly dismiss these first with the acknowledgment that most great Teachers have wrought works which, on the physical plane, appear as miracles in the sight of their contemporaries, but are known by occultists to be done by the exercise of powers possessed by all Initiates above a certain grade. The teachings He gave may also be acknowledged to be non-original; but where the student of Comparative Mythology thinks that he has proved that none is divinely inspired, when he shows that similar moral teachings fell from the lips of Manu, from the lips of the Buddha, from the lips of Jesus, the occultist says that certainly Jesus must have repeated the teachings of His predecessors, since He was a messenger from the same Lodge. The profound verities touching the divine and the human Spirit were as much truths twenty thousand years before Jesus was born in Palestine as after He was born; and to say that the world was left without such teaching, and that man was left in moral darkness from his beginnings to twenty centuries ago, is to say that there was a humanity without a Teacher, children without a Father, human souls crying for light into a darkness that gave them no answer — a conception as blasphemous of God as it is desperate for man, a conception contradicted by the appearance of every Sage, by the mighty literature, by the noble lives, in the thousands of ages ere the Christ came forth.

Recognising then in Jesus the great Master of the West, the leading Messenger of the Lodge to the western world, we must face the difficulty which has made havoc of this belief in the minds of many: Why are the festivals that commemorate events in the life of Jesus found in pre-Christian religions, and in them commemorate identical events in the lives of other Teachers?

Comparative Mythology, which has drawn public attention to this question in modern times, may be said to be about a century old, dating from the appearance of Dulaure's Histoire Abrégée de différents Cultes, of Dupuis' Origines de tous les Cultes, of Moor's Hindu Pantheon, and of Godfrey Higgins' Anacalypsis. These works were followed by a shoal of others, growing more scientific and rigid in their collection and comparison of facts, until it has become impossible for any educated person to even challenge the identities and similarities existing in every direction. Christians are not to be found, in these days, who are prepared to contend that Christian symbols, rites, and ceremonies are unique — except, indeed, among the ignorant. There we still behold simplicity of belief hand-in-hand with ignorance of facts; but outside this class we do not find even the most devout Christians alleging that Christianity has not very much in common with faiths older than itself. But it is well known that in the first centuries "after Christ" these likenesses were on all hands admitted, and that modern Comparative Mythology is only repeating with great precision that which was universally recognised in the Early Church. Justin Martyr, for instance, crowds his pages with references to the religions of his time, and if a modern assailant of Christianity would cite a number of cases in which Christian teachings are identical with those of elder religions, he can find no better guides than the apologists of the second century. They quote Pagan teachings, stories, and symbols, pleading that the very identity of the Christian with these should prevent the off hand rejection of the latter as in themselves incredible. A curious reason is, indeed, given for this identity, one that will scarcely find many adherents in modern days. Says Justin Martyr: "These who hand down the myths which the poets have made adduce no proof to the youths who learn them; and we proceed to demonstrate that they have been uttered by the influence of the wicked demons, to deceive and lead astray the human race. For having heard it proclaimed through the prophets that the Christ was to come, and that the ungodly among men were to be punished by fire, they put forward many to be called sons of Jupiter, under the impression that they would be able to produce in men the idea that the things which were said with regard to Christ were mere marvellous tales, like the things which were said by the poets". And the devils, indeed, having heard this washing published by the prophet, instigated those who enter their temples, and are about to approach them with libations and burnt offerings, also to sprinkle themselves; and they cause them also to wash themselves entirely as they depart". "Which [the Lord's Supper] the wicked devils have imitated in the mysteries of Mithras, commanding the same thing to be done". "For I myself, when I discovered the wicked disguise which the evil spirits had thrown around the divine doctrines of the Christians, to turn aside others from joining them, laughed".

These identities were thus regarded as the work of devils, copies of the Christian originals, largely circulated in the pre-Christian world with the object of prejudicing the reception of the truth when it came. There is a certain difficulty in accepting the earlier statements as copies and the later as originals, but without disputing with Justin Martyr whether the copies preceded the original or the original the copies, we may be content to accept his testimony as to the existence of these identities between the faith flourishing in the Roman empire of his time and the new religion he was engaged in defending.

Tertullian speaks equally plainly, stating the objection made in his days also to Christianity, that "the nations who are strangers to all understanding of spiritual powers, ascribe to their idols the imbuing of waters with the self-same efficacy". "So they do", he answers quite frankly, "but these cheat themselves with waters that are widowed. For washing is the channel through which they are initiated into some sacred rites of some notorious Isis or Mithra; and the Gods themselves they honour by washings .... At the Appollinarian and Eleusinian games they are baptised; and they presume that the effect of their doing that is the regeneration and the remission of the penalties due to their perjuries. Which fact, being acknowledged, we recognise here also the zeal of the devil rivalling the things of God, while we find him too practising baptism in his subjects". To solve the difficulty of these identities we must study the Mythic Christ, the Christ of the solar myths or legends, these myths being the pictorial forms in which certain profound truths were given to the world.

Now a "myth" is by no means what most people imagine it to be — a mere fanciful story erected on a basis of fact, or even altogether apart from fact. A myth is far truer than a history, for a history only gives a story of the shadows, whereas a myth gives a story of the substances that cast the shadows. As above so below; and first above and then below. There are certain great principles according to which our system is built; there are certain laws by which these principles are worked out in detail; there are certain Beings who embody the principles and whose activities are the laws;

there are hosts of inferior beings who act as vehicles for these activities, as agents, as instruments; there are the Egos of men intermingled with all these, performing their share of the great kosmic drama. These multifarious workers in the invisible worlds cast their shadows on physical matter, and these shadows are "things" — the bodies, the objects, that make up the physical universe. These shadows give but a poor idea of the objects that cast them, just as what we call shadows down here give but a poor idea of the objects that cast them; they are mere outlines, with blank darkness in lieu of details, and have only length and breadth, no depth.

History is an account, very imperfect and often distorted, of the dance of these shadows in the shadow-world of physical matter. Anyone who has seen, a clever Shadow-Play, and has compared what goes on behind the screen on which the shadows are cast with the movements of the shadows on the screen, may have a vivid idea of the illusory nature of the shadow-actions, and may draw therefrom several not misleading analogies.

Myth is an account of the movements of those who cast the shadows; and the language in which the account is given is what is called the language of symbols. Just as here we have words which stand for things — as the word "table" is a symbol for a recognised article of a certain kind — so do symbols stand for objects on higher planes. They are a pictorial alphabet, used by all myth-writers, and each has its recognised meaning. A symbol is used to signify a certain object just as words are used down here to distinguish one thing from another, and so a knowledge of symbols is necessary for the reading of a myth. For the original tellers of great myths are ever Initiates, who are accustomed to use the symbolic language, and who, of course, use symbols in their fixed and accepted meanings.

A symbol has a chief meaning, and then various subsidiary meanings related to that chief meaning. For instance, the Sun is the symbol of the Logos; that is its chief or primary significance. But it stands also for an incarnation of the Logos, or for any of the great Messengers who represent Him for the time, as an ambassador represents his King. High Initiates who are sent on special missions to incarnate among men and live with them for a time as Rulers or Teachers, would be designated by the symbol of the Sun; for though it is not their symbol in an individual sense, it is theirs in virtue of their office.

All those who are signified by this symbol have certain characteristics, pass through certain situations, perform certain activities, during their lives on earth. The Sun is the physical shadow, or body, as it is called, of the Logos; hence its yearly course in nature reflects His activity, in the partial way in which a shadow represents the activity of the object that casts it. The Logos, "the Son of God", descending into matter, has as shadow the annual course of the Sun, and the Sun-Myth tells it. Hence, again, an incarnation of the Logos, or one of His high ambassadors, will also represent that activity, shadow-like, in His body as a man. Thus will necessarily arise identities in the life-histories of these ambassadors. In fact, the absence of such identities would at once point out that the person concerned was not a full ambassador, and that his mission was of a lower order.

The Solar Myth, then, is a story which primarily representing the activity of the Logos, or Word, in the kosmos, secondarily embodies the life of one who is an incarnation of the Logos, or is one of His ambassadors. The Hero of the myth is usually represented as a God, or Demi-God, and his life, as will be understood by what has been said above, must be outlined by the course of the Sun, as the shadow of the Logos. The part of the course lived out during the human life is that which falls between the winter solstice and the reaching of the zenith in summer. The Hero is born at the winter solstice, dies at the spring equinox, and, conquering death, rises into mid-heaven.

The following remarks are interesting in this connection, though looking at myth in a more general way, as an allegory, picturing inner truths: "Alfred de Vigny has said that legend is frequently more true than history, because legend recounts not acts which are often incomplete and abortive, but the genius itself of great men and great nations. It is pre-eminently to the Gospel that this beautiful thought is applicable, for the Gospel is not merely the narration of what has been; it is the sublime narration of what is and what always will be. Ever will the Saviour of the world be adored by the kings of intelligence, represented by the Magi; ever will He multiply the eucharistic bread, to nourish and comfort our souls; ever, when we invoke Him in the night and the tempest, will He come to us walking on the waters, ever will He stretch forth His hand and make us pass over the crests of the billows; ever will He cure our distempers and give back light to our eyes; ever will He appear to His faithful, luminous and transfigured upon Tabor, interpreting the law of Moses and moderating the zeal of Elias".

We shall find that myths are very closely related to the Mysteries, for part of the Mysteries consisted in showing living pictures of the occurrences in the higher worlds that became embodied in myths. In fact in the Pseudo-Mysteries, mutilated fragments of the living pictures of the true Mysteries were represented by actors who acted out a drama, and many secondary myths are these dramas put into words.

The broad outlines of the story of the Sun-God are very clear, the eventful life of the Sun-God being spanned within the first six months of the solar year, the other six being employed in the general protecting and preserving. He is always born at the winter solstice, after the shortest day in the year, at the midnight of the 24th of December, when the sign Virgo is rising above the horizon; born as this sign is rising, he is born always of a virgin, and she remains a virgin after she has given birth to her Sun-Child, as the celestial Virgo remains unchanged and unsullied when the Sun comes forth from her in the heavens. Weak, feeble as an infant is he, born when the days are shortest and the nights are longest — we are on the north of the equatorial line — surrounded with perils in his infancy, and the reign of the darkness far longer than his in his early days. But he lives through all the threatening dangers, and the day lengthens towards the spring equinox, till the time comes for the crossing over, the crucifixion, the date varying with each year. The Sun-God is sometimes found sculptured within the circle of the horizon, with the head and feet touching the circle at north and south, and the outstretched hands at east and west — "He was crucified". After this he rises triumphantly and ascends into heaven, and ripens the corn and the grape, giving his very life to them to make their substance and through them to his worshippers. The God who is born at the dawning of December 25th is ever crucified at the spring equinox, and ever gives his life as food to his worshippers — these are among the most salient marks of the Sun-God. The fixity of the birth-date and the variableness of the death-date are full of significance, when we remember that the one is a fixed and the other a variable solar position. "Easter" is a movable event, calculated by the relative positions of sun and moon, an impossible way of fixing year by year the anniversary of a historical event, but a very natural and indeed inevitable way of calculating a solar festival. These changing dates do not point to the history of a man, but to the Hero of a solar myth.

These events are reproduced in the lives of the various Solar Gods, and antiquity teems with illustrations of them. Isis of Egypt like Mary of Bethlehem was our Immaculate Lady, Star of the Sea, Queen of Heaven, Mother of God. We see her in pictures standing on the crescent moon, star-crowned; she nurses her child Horus, and the cross appears on the back of the seat in which he sits on his mother's knee. The Virgo of the Zodiac is represented in ancient drawings as a woman suckling a child—the type of all future Madonnas with their divine Babes, showing the origin of the symbol. Devakî is likewise figured with the divine Krshna in her arms, as is Mylitta, or Istar, of Babylon, also with the recurrent crown of stars, and with her child Tammuz on her knee. Mercury and Aesculapius, Bacchus and Hercules, Perseus and the Dioscuri, Mithras and Zarathustra, were all of divine and human birth.

The relation of the winter solstice to Jesus is also significant. The birth of Mithras was celebrated in the winter solstice with great rejoicings, and Horus was also then born: "His birth is one of the greatest mysteries of the [Egyptian] religion. Pictures representing it appeared on the walls of temples. . . . He was the child of Deity. At Christmas time, or that answering to our festival, his image was brought out of the sanctuary with peculiar ceremonies, as the image of the infant Bambino is still brought out and exhibited at Rome".

On the fixing of the 25th December as the birthday of Jesus, Williamson has the following: "All Christians know that the 25th December is now the recognised festival of the birth of Jesus, but few are aware that this has not always been so. There have been, it is said, one hundred and thirty-six different dates fixed on by different Christian sects. Lightfoot gives it as 15th September, others as in February or August. Epiphanius mentions two sects, one celebrating it in June, the other in July. The matter was finally settled by Pope Julius I, in 337 A. D., and S. Chrysostom, writing in 390, says : ' On this day [.i.e., 25th December] also the birth of Christ was lately fixed at Rome, in order that while the heathen were busy with their ceremonies [the Brumalia, in honour of Bacchus] the Christians might perform their rites undisturbed.' Gibbon in his Decline and Fall of the Roman Empire, writes: ' The [Christian] Romans, as ignorant as their brethren of the real date of his [Christ's birth] fixed the solemn festival to the 25th December, the Brumalia or winter solstice, when the Pagans annually celebrated the birth of the Sun.' King, in his Gnostics and Their Remains, also says: ' The ancient festival held on the 25th December in honour of the birthday of the Invincible One, and celebrated by the great games at the Circus, was afterwards transferred to the commemoration of the birth of Christ, the precise date of which many of the Fathers confess was then unknown;' while at the present day Canon Farrar writes that 'all attempts to discover the month and day of the nativity are useless. No data whatever exist to enable us to determine them with even approximate accuracy.' From the foregoing it is apparent that the great festival of the winter solstice has been celebrated during past ages, and in widely separated lands, in honour of the birth of a God, who is almost invariably alluded to as a ' Saviour,' and whose mother is referred to as a pure virgin. The striking resemblances, too, which have been instanced not only in the birth but in the life of so many of these Saviour-Gods are far too numerous to be accounted for by any mere coincidence".

In the case of the Lord Buddha we may see how a myth attaches itself to a historical personage. The story of His life is well known, and in the current Indian accounts the birth-story is simple and human. But in the Chinese account He is born of a virgin, Mâyâdevi, the archaic myth finding in Him a new Hero.

Williamson also tells us that fires were and are lighted on the 25th December on the hills among Keltic peoples, and these are still known among the Irish and the Scotch Highlanders as Bheil or Baaltinne, the fires thus bearing the name of Bel, Bal, or Baal, their ancient Deity, the Sun-God, though now lighted in honour of Christ.

Rightly considered, the Christmas festival should take on new elements of rejoicing and of sacredness, when the lovers of Christ see in it the repetition of an ancient solemnity, see it stretching all the world over, and far, far back into dim antiquity; so that the Christmas bells are ringing throughout human history, and sound musically out of the far-off night of time. Not in exclusive possession, but in universal acceptance, is found the hall-mark of truth.

The death-date, as said above, is not a fixed one, like the birth-date. The date of the death is calculated by the relative positions of Sun and Moon at the spring equinox, varying with each year, and the death-date of each Solar Hero is found to be celebrated in this connection. The animal adopted as the symbol of the Hero is the sign of the Zodiac in which the Sun is at the vernal equinox of his age, and this varies with the precession of the equinoxes. Oannes of Assyria had the sign of Pisces, the Fish, and is thus figured. Mithra is in Taurus, and, therefore, rides on a Bull, and Osiris was worshipped as Osiris-Apis, or Serapis, the Bull. Merodach of Babylon was worshipped as a Bull, as was Astarte of Syria. When the Sun is in the sign of Aries, the Ram or Lamb, we have Osiris again as Ram, and so also Astarte, and Jupiter Ammon, and it is this same animal that became the symbol of Jesus — the Lamb of God. The use of the Lamb as His symbol, often leaning on a cross, is common in the sculptures of the catacombs. On this Williamson says: "In the course of time the Lamb was represented on the cross, but it was not until the sixth synod of Constantinople, held about the year 680, that it was ordained that instead of the ancient symbol, the figure of a manfastened to a cross should be represented. This canon was confirmed by Pope Adrian I". The very ancient Pisces is also assigned to Jesus, and He is thus pictured in the catacombs.

The death and resurrection of the Solar Hero at or about the vernal equinox is as wide-spread as his birth at the winter solstice. Osiris was then slain by Typhon, and He is pictured on the circle of the horizon, with outstretched arms, as if crucified — a posture originally of benediction, not of suffering. The death of Tammuz was annually bewailed at the spring equinox in Babylonia and Syria, as were Adonis in Syria and Greece, and Attis in Phrygia, pictured "as a man fastened with a lamb at the foot". Mithras' death was similarly celebrated in Persia, and that of Bacchus and Dionysius — one and the same — in Greece. In Mexico the same idea reappears, as usual accompanied with the cross.

In all these cases the mourning for the death is immediately followed by the rejoicing over the resurrection, and on this it is interesting to notice hat the name of Easter has been traced to the virgin-mother of the slain Tammuz, Ishtar.

It is interesting also to notice that the fast preceding the death at the vernal equinox, — the modern Lent — is found in Mexico, Egypt, Persia, Babylon, Assyria, Asia Minor, in some cases definitely for forty days.

In the Pseudo-Mysteries, the Sun-God story was dramatised, and in the ancient Mysteries it was lived by the Initiate, and hence the solar "myths" and the great facts of Initiation became interwoven together. Hence when the Master Christ became the Christ of the Mysteries, the legends of the older Heroes of those Mysteries gathered round Him, and the stories were again recited with the latest divine Teacher as the representative of the Logos in the Sun. Then the festival of His nativity became the immemorial date when the Sun was born of the Virgin, when the midnight sky was filled with the rejoicing hosts of the celestials, and Very early, very early, Christ was born.

As the great legend of the Sun gathered round Him, the sign of the Lamb became that of His crucifixion as the sign of the Virgin had become that of His birth. We have seen that the Bull was sacred to Mithras and the Fish to Oannes, and that the Lamb was sacred to Christ, and for the same reason; it was the sign of the spring equinox, at the period of history in which He crossed the great circle of the horizon, was "crucified in space".

These Sun myths, ever recurring throughout the ages, with a different name for their Hero in each new recension, cannot pass unrecognised by the student, though they may naturally and rightly be ignored by the devotee; and when they are used as a weapon to mutilate or destroy the majestic figure of the Christ, they must be met, not by denying the facts, but by understanding the deeper meaning of the stories, the spiritual truths that the legends expressed under a veil.

Why have these legends mingled with the history of Jesus, and crystallised round Him, as a historical personage ? These are really the stories not of a particular individual named Jesus but of the universal Christ; of a Man who symbolised a Divine Being, and who represented a fundamental truth in nature; a Man who filled a certain office and held a certain characteristic position towards humanity; standing towards humanity in a special relationship, renewed age after age, as generation succeeded generation, as race gave way to race. Hence He was, as are all such, the "Son of Man", a peculiar and distinctive title, the title of an office, not of an individual. The Christ of the Solar Myth was the Christ of the Mysteries, and we find the secret of the mythic in the mystic Christ.

THE MYSTIC CHRIST

We now approach that deeper side of the Christ story that gives it its real hold upon the hearts of men. We approach that perennial life which bubbles up from an unseen source, and so baptises its representative with its lucent flood that human hearts cling round the Christ, and feel that they could almost more readily reject the apparent facts of history than deny that which they intuitively feel to be a vital, an essential truth of the higher life. We draw near the sacred portal of the Mysteries, and lift a corner of the veil that hides the sanctuary.

We have seen that, go back as far as we may into antiquity, we find everywhere recognised the existence of a hidden teaching, a secret doctrine, given under strict and exacting conditions to approved candidates by the Masters of Wisdom. Such candidates were initiated into "The Mysteries" — a name that covers in antiquity, as we have seen, all that was most spiritual in religion, all that was most profound in philosophy, all that was most valuable in science. Every great Teacher of antiquity passed through the Mysteries and the greatest were the Hierophants of the Mysteries; each who came forth into the world to speak of the invisible worlds had passed through the portal of Initiation and had learned the secret of the Holy Ones from Their own lips: each who came forth came forth with the same story, and the solar myths are all versions of this story, identical in their essential features, varying only in their local colour.

This story is primarily that of the descent of the Logos into matter, and the Sun-God is aptly His symbol, since the Sun is His body, and He is often described as "He that dwelleth in the Sun". In one aspect, the Christ of the Mysteries is the Logos descending into matter, and the great Sun-Myth is the popular teaching of this sublime truth. As in previous cases, the Divine Teacher, who brought the Ancient Wisdom and republished it in the world, was regarded as a special manifestation of the Logos, and the Jesus of the Churches was gradually draped with the stories which belonged to this great One; thus He became identified, in Christian nomenclature, with the Second Person in the Trinity, the Logos, or Word of God, and the salient events recounted in the myth of the Sun-God became the salient events of the story of Jesus, regarded as the incarnate Deity, the "mythic Christ". As in the macrocosm, the kosmos, the Christ of the Mysteries represents the Logos, the Second Person in the Trinity, so in the microcosm, man, does He represent the second aspect of the Divine Spirit in man — hence called in man "the Christ". The second aspect of the Christ of the Mysteries is then the life of the Initiate, the life which is entered on at the first great Initiation, at which the Christ is born in man, and after which He develops in man. To make this quite intelligible, we must consider the conditions imposed on the candidate for Initiation, and the nature of the Spirit in man.

Only those could be recognised as candidates for Initiation who were already good as men count goodness, according to the strict measure of the law. Pure, holy, without defilement, clean from sin, living without transgression — such were some of the descriptive phrases used of them. Intelligent also must they be, of well-developed and well-trained minds. The evolution carried on in the world life after life, developing and mastering the powers of the mind, the emotions, and the moral sense, learning through exoteric religions, practising the discharge of duties, seeking to help and lift others — all this belongs to the ordinary life of an evolving man. When all this is done, the man has become "a good man", the

Chrêstos of the Greeks, and this he must be ere he can become the Christos, the Anointed. Having accomplished the exoteric good life, he becomes a candidate for the esoteric life, and enters on the preparation for Initiation, which consists in the fulfilment of certain conditions.

These conditions mark out the attributes he is to acquire, and while he is labouring to create these, he is sometimes said to be treading the Probationary Path, the Path which leads up to the "Strait Gate", beyond which is the "Narrow Way", or the "Path of Holiness", the " Way of the Cross". He is not expected to develop these attributes perfectly, but he must have made some progress in all of them, ere the Christ can be born in him. He must prepare a pure home for that Divine Child who is to develop within him.

The first of these attributes — they are all mental and moral — is Discrimination; this means that the aspirant must begin to separate in his mind the Eternal from the Temporary, the Real from the Unreal, the True from the False, the Heavenly from the Earthly. "The things which are seen are temporal", says the Apostle; "but the things which are not seen are eternal". Men are constantly living under the glamour of the seen, and are blinded by it to the unseen. The aspirant must learn to discriminate between them, so that what is unreal to the world may become real to him, and that which is real to the world may to him become unreal, for thus only is it possible to "walk by faith, not by sight". And thus also must a man become one of those of whom the Apostle says that they "are of full age, even those who by reason of use have their senses exercised to discern both good and evil". Next, this sense of unreality must breed in him Disgust with the unreal and the fleeting, the mere husks of life, unfit to satisfy hunger, save the hunger of swine. This stage is described in the emphatic language of Jesus: "If any man come to me, and hate not his father, and mother, and wife, and children, and brethren, and sisters, yea, and his own life also, he cannot be my disciple". Truly a "hard saying", and yet out of this hatred will spring a deeper, truer, love, and the stage may not be escaped on the way to the Strait Gate. Then the aspirant must learn Control of thoughts, and this will lead to Control of actions, the thought being, to the inner eye, the same as the action: "Whosoever looketh on a woman to lust after her, hath committed adultery with her already in his heart". He must acquire Endurance, for they who aspire to tread "the Way of the Cross" will have to brave long and bitter sufferings, and they must be able to endure, "as seeing Him who is invisible". He must add to these Tolerance, if he would be the child of Him who "maketh His sun to rise on the evil, and on the good, and sendeth rain on the just and on the unjust", the disciple of Him who bade His apostles not to forbid a man to use His name because he did not follow with them. Further, he must acquire the Faith to which nothing is impossible, and the Balance which is described by the Apostle. Lastly, he must seek only "those things which are above", and long to reach the beatitude of the vision of and union with God. When a man has wrought these qualities into his character he is regarded as fit for Initiation, and the Guardians of the Mysteries will open for him the Strait Gate. Thus, but thus only, he becomes the prepared candidate.

Now, the Spirit in man is the gift of the Supreme God, and contains within itself the three aspects of the Divine Life — Intelligence, Love, Will — being the Image of God. As it evolves, it first develops the aspect of Intelligence, develops the intellect, and this evolution is effected in the ordinary life in the world. To have done this to a high point, accompanying it with moral development, brings the evolving man to the condition of the candidate. The second aspect of the Spirit is that of Love, and the evolution of that is the evolution of the Christ. In the true Mysteries this evolution is undergone — the disciple's life is the Mystery Drama, and the Great Initiations mark its stages. In the Mysteries performed on the physical plane these used to be dramatically represented, and the ceremonies followed in many respects "the pattern" ever shown forth "on the Mount", for they were the shadows in a deteriorating age of the mighty Realities in the spiritual world.

The Mystic Christ, then, is twofold — the Logos, the Second Person of the Trinity, descending into matter, and the Love, or second, aspect of the unfolding Divine Spirit in man. The one represents kosmic processes carried on in the past and is the root of the Solar Myth; the other represents a process carried on in the individual, the concluding stage of his human evolution, and added many details in the Myth. Both of these have contributed to the Gospel story, and together form the Image of the "Mystic Christ".

Let us consider first the kosmic Christ, Deity becoming enveloped in matter, the becoming incarnate of the Logos, the clothing of God in "flesh".

When the matter which is to form our solar system is separated off from the infinite ocean of matter which fills space, the Third Person of the Trinity — the Holy Spirit — pours His Life into this matter to vivify it, that it may presently take form. It is then drawn together, and form is given to it by the life of the Logos, the Second Person of the Trinity, who sacrifices Himself by putting on the limitations of matter, becoming the "Heavenly Man", in whose Body all forms exist, of whose Body all forms are part. This was the kosmic story, dramatically shown in the Mysteries — in the true Mysteries seen as it occurred in space, in the physical plane Mysteries represented by magical or other means, and in some parts by actors.

These processes are very distinctly stated in the Bible; when the "Spirit of God moved upon the face of the waters" in the darkness that was "upon the face of the deep", the great deep of matter showed no forms, it was void, inchoate. Form was given by the Logos, the Word, of whom it is written that "all things were made by Him; and without Him was not anything made that was made." C. W. Leadbeater has well put it: "The result of this first great outpouring [the 'moving' of the Spirit] is the quickening of that wonderful and glorious vitality which pervades all matter (inert though it may seem to our dim physical eyes), so that the atoms of the various planes develop, when electrified by it, all sorts of previously latent attractions and repulsions, and enter into combinations of all kinds".

Only when this work of the Spirit has been done can the Logos, the kosmic Mystic Christ, take on Himself the clothing of matter, entering in very truth the Virgin's womb, the womb of Matter as yet virgin, unproductive. This matter had been vivified by the Holy Spirit, who, overshadowing the Virgin, poured into it His life, thus preparing it to receive the life of the Second Logos, who took this matter as the vehicle for His energies. This is the becoming incarnate of the Christ, the taking flesh — "Thou did'st not despise the Virgin's womb".

In the Latin and English translations of the original Greek text of the Nicene Creed, the phrase which describes this phase of the descent has changed the prepositions and so changed the sense. The original ran: "and was incarnate of the Holy Ghost and the Virgin Mary", whereas he translation reads : " and was incarnate by the Holy Ghost of the Virgin Mary." The Christ "takes form not of the ' Virgin' matter alone, but of matter which is already instinct and pulsating with the life of the Third Logos, so that both the life and the matter surround Him as a vesture."

This is the descent of the Logos into matter, described as the birth of the Christ of a Virgin, and this, in the Solar Myth, becomes the birth of the Sun-God as the sign Virgo rises.

Then come the early workings of the Logos in matter, aptly typified by the infancy of the myth. To all the feebleness of infancy His majestic powers bow themselves, letting but little play forth on the tender forms they ensoul. Matter imprisons, seems as though threatening to slay, its infant King, whose glory is veiled by the limitations He has assumed. Slowly He shapes it towards high ends, and lifts it into manhood, and then stretches Himself on the cross of matter that He may pour forth from that cross alt the powers of His surrendered life. This is the Logos of whom Plato said that He was in the figure of a cross on the universe; this is the Heavenly Man, standing in space, with arms outstretched in blessing; this is the Christ crucified, whose death on the cross of matter fills all matter with His life. Dead He seems and buried out of sight, but He rises again clothed in the very matter in which He seemed to perish, and carries up His body of now radiant matter into heaven, where it receives the downpouring life of the Father, and becomes the vehicle of man's immortal life. For it is the life of the Logos which forms the garment of the Soul in man, and He gives it that men may live through the ages and grow to the measure of His own stature. Truly are we clothed in Him, first materially and then spiritually. He sacrificed Himself to bring many sons into glory, and He is with us always, even to the end of the age.

The crucifixion of Christ, then, is part of the great kosmic sacrifice, and the allegorical representation of this in the physical

Mysteries, and the sacred symbol of the crucified man in space, became materialised into an actual death by crucifixion, and a crucifix bearing a dying human form; then this story, now the story of a man, was attached to the Divine Teacher, Jesus, and became the story of His physical death, while the birth from a Virgin, the danger-encircled infancy, the resurrection and ascension, became also incidents in His human life. The Mysteries disappeared, but their grandiose and graphic representations of the kosmic work of the Logos encircled and uplifted the beloved figure of the Teacher of Judaea, and the kosmic Christ of the Mysteries, with the lineaments of the Jesus of history, thus became the central Figure of the Christian Church.

But even this was not all; the last touch of fascination is added to the Christ-story by the fact that there is another Christ of the Mysteries, close and dear to the human heart — the Christ of the human Spirit, the Christ who is in every one of us, is born and lives, is crucified, rises from the dead, and ascends into heaven, in every suffering and triumphant "Son of Man".

The life-story of every Initiate into the true, the heavenly Mysteries, is told in its salient features in the Gospel biography. For this reason, S. Paul speaks as we have seen of the birth of the Christ in the disciple, and of His evolution and His full stature therein. Every man is a potential Christ, and the unfolding of the Christ-life in a man follows the outline of the Gospel story in its striking incidents, which we have seen to be universal, and not particular.

There are five great Initiations in the life of a Christ, each one marking a stage in the unfolding of the Life of Love. They are given now, as of old, and the last marks the final triumph of the Man who has developed into Divinity, who has transcended humanity, and has become a Saviour of the world.

Let us trace this life-story, ever newly repeated in spiritual experience, and see the Initiate living out the life of the Christ.

At the first great Initiation the Christ is born in the disciple; it is then that he realises for the first time in himself the outpouring of the divine Love, and experiences that marvellous change which makes him feel himself to be one with all that lives. This is the "Second Birth", and at that birth the heavenly ones rejoice, for he is born into " the kingdom of heaven", as one of the " little ones," as "a little child " — the names ever given to the new initiates. Such is the meaning of the words of Jesus, that a man must become a little child to enter into the Kingdom. It is significantly said in some of the early Christian writers that Jesus was "born in a cave" — the "stable" of the gospel narrative; the "Cave of Initiation" is a well-known ancient phrase, and the Initiate is ever born therein; over that cave "where the young child" is, burns the "Star of Initiation", the Star that ever shines forth in the East when a Child-Christ is born. Every such child is surrounded by perils and menaces, strange dangers that befall not other babes; for he is anointed with the chrism of the second birth and the Dark Powers of the unseen world ever seek his undoing. Despite all trials, however, he grows into manhood, for the Christ once born can never perish, the Christ once beginning to develop can never fail in his evolution; his fair life expands and grows, ever-increasing in wisdom and in spiritual stature, until the time comes for the second great Initiation, the Baptism of the Christ by Water and the Spirit, that gives him the powers necessary for the Teacher, who is to go forth and labour in the world as "the beloved Son".

Then there descends upon him in rich measure the divine Spirit, and the glory of the unseen Father pours down its pure radiance on him; but from that scene of blessing is he led by the Spirit into the wilderness and is once more exposed to the ordeal of fierce temptations. For now the powers of the Spirit are unfolding themselves in him, and the Dark Ones strive to lure him from his path by these very powers, bidding him use them for his own helping instead of resting on his Father in patient trust. In the swift, sudden transitions which test his strength and faith, the whisper of the embodied Tempter follows the voice of the Father, and the burning sands of the wilderness scorch the feet erstwhile laved in the cool waters of the holy river. Conqueror over these temptations he passes into the world of men to use for their helping the powers he would not put forth for his own needs, and he who would not turn one stone to bread for the stilling of his own cravings feeds "five thousand men, besides women and children", with a few loaves.

Into his life of ceaseless service conies another brief period of glory, when he ascends "a high mountain apart" — the sacred Mount of Initiation. There he is transfigured and there meets some of his great Forerunners, the Mighty Ones of old who trod where he now is treading. He passes thus the third great Initiation, and then the shadow of his coming Passion falls on him, and he steadfastly sets his face to go to Jerusalem — repelling the tempting words of one of his disciples — Jerusalem, where awaits him the baptism of the Holy Ghost and of Fire. After the Birth, the attack by Herod; after the Baptism, the temptation in the wilderness; after the Transfiguration, the setting forth towards the last stage of the Way of the Cross. Thus is triumph ever followed by ordeal, until the goal is reached.

Still grows the life of love, ever fuller and more perfect, the Son of Man shining forth more clearly as the Son of God, until the time draws near for his final battle, and the fourth great Initiation leads him in triumph into Jerusalem, into sight of Gethsemane and Calvary. He is now the Christ ready to be offered, ready for the sacrifice on the cross- He is now to face the bitter agony in the Garden, where even his chosen ones sleep while he wrestles with his mortal anguish, and for a moment prays that the cup may pass from his lips; but the strong will triumphs and he stretches out his hand to take and drink, and in his loneliness an angel comes to him and strengthens him, as angels are wont to do when they see a Son of Man bending beneath his load of agony. The drinking of the bitter cup of betrayal, of desertion, of denial, meets him as he goes forth, and alone amid his jeering foes he passes to his last fierce trial. Scourged by physical pain, pierced by cruel thorns of suspicion, stripped of his fair garments of purity in the eyes of the world, left in the hands of his foes, deserted apparently by God and man, he endures patiently all that befalls him, wistfully looking in his last extremity for aid. Left still to suffer, crucified, to die to the life of form, to surrender all life that belongs to the lower world, surrounded by triumphant foes who mock him, the last horror of great darkness envelopes him, and in the darkness he meets all the forces of evil; his inner vision is blinded, he finds himself alone, utterly alone, till the strong heart, sinking in despair, cries out to the Father who seems to have abandoned him, and the human soul faces, in uttermost loneliness, the crushing agony of apparent defeat. Yet, summoning all the strength of the "unconquerable spirit", the lower life is yielded up, its death is willingly embraced, the body of desire is abandoned, and the Initiate "descends into hell", that no region of the universe he is to help may remain untrodden by him, that none may be too outcast to be reached by his all-embracing love. And then springing upwards from the darkness, he sees the light once more, feels himself again as the Son, inseparable from the Father whose he is, rises to the life that knows no ending, radiant in the consciousness of death faced and overcome, strong to help to the uttermost every child of man, able to pour out his life into every struggling soul. Among his disciples he remains awhile to teach, unveiling to them the mysteries of the spiritual worlds, preparing them also to tread the path he has trodden, until, the earth-life over, he ascends to the Father, and, in the fifth great Initiation, becomes the Master triumphant, the link between God and man.

Such was the story lived through in the true Mysteries of old and now, and dramatically portrayed in symbols in the physical plane Mysteries, half veiled, half shown. Such is the Christ of the Mysteries in His dual aspect, Logos and man, kosmic and individual. Is it any wonder that this story, dimly felt, even when unknown, by the mystic, has woven itself into the heart, and served as an inspiration to all noble living ? The Christ of the human heart is, for the most part, Jesus seen as the mystic human Christ, struggling, suffering, dying, finally triumphant, the Man in whom humanity is seen crucified and risen, whose victory is the promise of victory to every one who, like Him, is faithful through death and beyond — the Christ who can never be forgotten while He is born again and again in humanity, while the world needs Saviours, and Saviours give themselves for men.

www.ingramcontent.com/pod-product-compliance
Lightning Source LLC
LaVergne TN
LVHW050947080826
845145LV00004B/1442

* 9 7 8 1 6 3 1 1 8 5 3 3 5 *